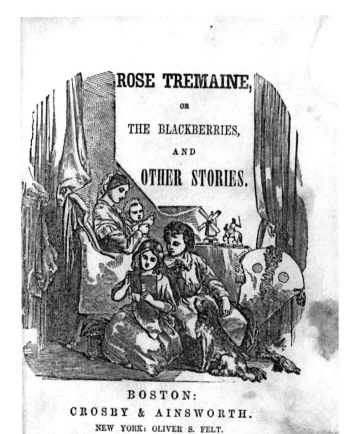

ROSE TREMAINE,

OR

THE BLACKBERRIES,

AND

OTHER STORIES.

BOSTON:

CROSBY & AINSWORTH.

NEW YORK: OLIVER S. FELT.

1866.

Printing Statement:

Due to the very old age and scarcity of this book,
many of the pages may be hard to read due to the
blurring of the original text, possible missing pages,
missing text, dark backgrounds and other issues
beyond our control.

Because this is such an important and rare work, we
believe it is best to reproduce this book regardless of
its original condition.

Thank you for your understanding.

STORIES.

THE BLACKBERRIES.

In Cumberland there are, as everybody knows, a number of beautiful lakes; some are large, and others small, but most of them have pretty little woody islands dotted over their surface, and fairy bays and headlands on their shores. In the numerous peaceful valleys which slope from the lofty hills to the water's edge, are built pretty villages and hamlets, and many handsome houses are

(5)

scattered about in the woods, and on the promontories above them.

In one of these vales was a village more secluded than ordinary from the world's notice. Its inhabitants were chiefly composed of farmers, and the laborers whom they employed. Among the latter, there was nowhere to be found a more industrious and clever, or more cheerful man, than Edward Trevaine; he was always in request wherever work requiring more than usual talent and knowledge was to be done, and consequently he gained more money than most of his companions; this might have made them jealous, had he not been ever ready to help them in sorrow or want to the best of his ability. Trevaine was also blessed by the pos-

session of a good wife, and one sweet
little daughter, who was the pride and
delight, not only of her parents, but of
the whole village. Mothers told their
children to follow the example of little
Rose, and fathers said how happy the
Tremaines must be in her good conduct.
At school her lessons were ready first,
and repeated the most perfectly; at play
she was always kind and obliging, and
never quarrelsome; and at home she
was obedient and affectionate; never
giving trouble, but watching for oppor-
tunities to assist her kind mother in her
household work; but still Rose was not
perfectly good; she used sometimes,
though very seldom, to do what she was

not told to do; and I will give you an account of one of these sad occasions.

Rose returned from school one bright morning, in the beginning of autumn, with her neat little book-bag on her arm, and her sweet face beaming with happiness. She ran across the well-stocked garden, and entering the cottage threw her arms round her mother's neck, and kissed her.

"Have you been good this morning, darling?" was the kind question with which she was greeted.

"Yes, mother! and now I want you to grant me a favor! Will you?"

"What is it dear?"

"May I go into the field above the sand bay, to see if the blackberries are ripe? I won't eat many, but will bring them home to you, my own dear mother; and if I get a great quantity you will make a pudding for Sunday, and father will be so pleased!"

"Yes," replied her mother, "you may go dear; but mind you do not go beyond the first field, or I shall not know where to find you for dinner."

So Rose put her books in the cupboard, and, after promising obedience, took her little basket and bounded from the house. She soon reached the desired spot, and hunted all over the hedges and brambles she could find, but there was no ripe fruit on them; and she picked a few flowers, wandered on towards the stile that led into the next field; this was quickly reached, and Rose looked over it. She stretched out her head to see if any blackberries were ripe there, and perceived, not within reach of where she stood, but yet so near, that if she only just got over the gate she could obtain them, a large bunch of the finest she had seen that day.

"Oh," thought Rose, "I must have these; I will only cross the stile and come back again. Mother's reason for telling me not to go, was in case she should not be able to find me." And in one moment she had disobeyed, and was standing on the other side of the hedge, eagerly plucking the berries. When they were gathered, Rose looked further, and at about half a dozen yards' distance

were a great many more, so she said to
herself,—"Well, just these, and I will
go back;" but when these were also de-
posited in her basket, she was tempted
afresh, and I am sorry to say, strayed
from bramble to bramble, till she had
reached the opposite stile that led into a
third field; here she again peeped, and a
bunch of nuts tempted her to transgress
still further, and the little girl yielded,
and went after them. She picked the
nuts from the tree, and looked around
her; the hedge was formed of nut trees
and brambles, and she thought, that as
she had gone into the enclosure, she
might as well get all she could; and she
walked on, pulling every nut or berry
that she saw. By and by she reached a

part of a fence which joined a wild wood, that covered the sides and summit of one of the highest hills on the borders of the lake; just before her was a gap that had been made by the village children, when on nutting excursions, and inside the edge of the forest was a beautiful bed of wild strawberries.

"Oh!" exclaimed the little girl, "how beautiful they look! I will pick them, and then I must run back as fast as I can." So she scrambled through the hedge, and began to gather the fruit in great haste; but the bank was a long one, and led some way into the wood; besides, the nuts hung in clusters around, and Rose was tempted on, till at last she lost the path.

There were a great many little roads through the wood, and she ran about looking and longing for the one that led to the village, but she could not find it. Then she called to her mother as loud as she could, but her mother could neither hear nor answer her; so at last she sat down on the mossy-root of a large oak tree, and cried very bitterly. "Oh dear!" she said, "how unhappy am I! What will become of me? I shall never find my way out of the wood, and the gipsies will take me away." And her tears flowed afresh. But soon Rose felt hungry; she had not eaten since her breakfast, and it was now far advanced in the afternoon; so she took the wild fruits that had seduced her into the wood, and made an unsubstantial meal of them. After resting a little she again set out on her wanderings; but turn where she would the paths only led further into the forest. Poor Rose now began to be very frightened and very sad, and she wished she had staid in the first field and done as her mother had bidden her.

She walked a long way further, and saw that the sun was getting very low, and then she stood still by the side of a little spring of water that welled up from beneath a bit of gray rock, thickly covered with yellow lichen, and over which the bare and knotty roots of the trees were hanging. Rose waited and watched till the sun was gone, and darkness had spread its mantle over the quiet earth.

She did not heed the little birds that were twittering " Good night" to one another in the branches, or the merry chirp of the grasshoppers come out for their evening stroll; but she thought of her dear mother, and her little heart was bursting with its load of grief and guilt. It was useless to go further, and Rose's feet were swollen already with walking; so she sat down by the gray stone and gazed on the tiny pool formed by the crystal spring. As she watched it she saw the reflected image of a star trembling on its mirror-like surface, and Rose raised her weeping eyes to the blue heaven above. There she saw the countless lamps of light burning in their glory; and as her thoughts reverted to the God who had created them, she bent her knees and fervently supplicated mercy and protection. She rose calm and comforted, and then laid herself down on the green moss and grass to rest before she again attempted to reach the village.

Meantime all was grief and sorrow in the hamlet. Mrs. Trevaine went to call Rose, and found she was not in the first field; she searched for her in those adjoining, but in vain. She then flew back to the village, and asked her neighbors if they had seen her lost child. But all said "No:" and the terrified mother became frantic with anxiety. Her husband now returned from his work with the other men, and on hearing the sorrowful tale, they all agreed to go in quest of the the little truant.

Accordingly, they formed into numerous parties, and took different routes, agreeing to return to the village by an appointed hour, so that if none of them had found Rose they might consult about further plans of search. The time so anxiously looked for by the agonised mother at length arrived, and the men were discovered approaching on their return. The children ran towards them to learn news of their lost companion, but did not hasten back to their mothers, for they had no joyful tidings to communicate. In a few minutes the various parties had met on the village green, under the branches of the aged lime tree; and,

2

after comparing their adventures, and echoing the tale of disappointment from mouth to mouth, Edward and a few of the kindest of his neighbors arranged to make one more trial that night in the wood, and armed with stout sticks and lanterns they set out, accompanied by the prayers of all who remained behind. After wandering and searching for some time, without obtaining so much even as a trace of the lost child, one of the men, who was separated some distance from the rest, hailed them with the cry of "Found, found!" All hurried to the sound of the voice, and there, lying on the green moss, was little Rose in a troubled sleep. Her father caught her in his arms, and, with a loud scream, the

little creature recognized him in the un-
certain light, and buried her burning
face on his shoulder. Questions were
rapidly put to the poor child, and an-
swered by her with shame and sorrow
and the men prepared to carry her back
to the village in triumph. Rose, in the
meantime, told her father that she was
dreaming at the very moment he awoke
her that a wolf was eating her up, and
said she was trying to pray to God to
save her from it. In the course of an
hour they were descried from the village
green, and this time the little folks who
flew to meet them vied with each other
in trying who should first reach the
anxious group of men and women, and
tell them that dear Rose was safe. The

pastor, who was occupied in his study, came out to meet them, and after the first delirium of joy was over, he called upon his flock to return thanks to God for the preservation of the beloved child. What words can picture the beauty of the scene which followed? There, on the soft grass under the old tree, knelt many an aged man and woman, many a hale, hearty laborer and his wife, and many a light-hearted child. All were hushed in solemn silence, while their venerated minister, with Rose kneeling beside him, implored the pardon of God for her fault, and His blessing upon her, and that His watchful eye might be over every one then before Him, to protect them from all evil and save them from sin. He then called on the assembly to sing a hymn of praise, and afterwards dismissed them with his blessing. The benighted traveller started on his road to hear the notes of thanksgiving swelling on the moonlit air, and paused and hung on the notes till they died away, when, with a full heart and chastening sigh, he resumed his way, wondering whence those voices could have arisen, so sweet, so full of meaning were the souls who sung.

THE WAX DOLL.

OFTEN when a little girl, have I stood at shop-windows, gazing at wax dolls. They seemed far beyond my reach, for I had no money to purchase them. And yet they looked so smiling, it was hard to leave them and go home to my alabaster doll, Sally, whose beauty had long since departed.

Sometimes carriages would before the shop-doors where I was peeping in, bearing richly dressed ladies, and little girls, looking as fine as the wax dolls. Then the steps were let down with a great slam, and they tripping along entered

(22)

the shop. They asked for wax dolls, and I must needs look on to see which was the chosen one. A little girl would hold it forth so pleased, that I had to be pleased too as she rustled by me in her silk dress and sprang into the carriage, not even knowing that I was standing near. But as she passed, I could hear her mama say anxiously, sometimes,—

"Take care, my daughter, do not hurt your new doll."

I went home and was soon consoled by my alabaster baby, Sally, which I held without fear.

Once I went to visit a little girl, who had a splendid wax doll sent to her from her uncle in London. But where do you think it was? It was in a glass case. I was allowed to look at its red cheeks, and curling hair, and satin slippers, and gay sash, but not to touch her. A very careful, big person, could take her out of the case, and pull a wire that opened and shut her eyes, but no child was allowed to pull that mysterious wire. What great wonder took hold of my mind when I saw those eyes close and open! But I went home to my plain doll Sally more satisfied than ever. I kissed her and tossed her in the air, and when she came down head first, I laughed, and said,

"It is better to have you, Sally, though you are not so pretty, than a wax doll in a case!

Since I became a woman I have seen

many wax dolls,—gay, happy-looking things. Some were new-year's gifts; some, birth-day presents; and the little children to whom they were presented seemed gay and happy too: but once I saw a wax doll in a coffin, and I will tell you how it was.

I knew a little boy whom I shall call Angel, because he is now an angel in heaven. He was like a beautiful doll when he was alive, for he had large blue eyes, and light curling hair, and a round, smooth face, and a dimpled smile.

This little boy had a friend about three years old. I will call her Cherub, because she, too, is now a cherub in heaven. She did not look like a doll; her features were not so regular as the boy's, but

there was something wonderfully sweet
in her darkly bright eyes, that made you
think of light and love; and then she
sang like one of Heaven's children before
her time.

Well, Angel was taken ill, and after a
few days of suffering he said,—

"Mama, I wish you to get my own
money, that is in my little purse, and
buy a wax doll for Cherub."

His mama said—"Yes, my child;"
but before she could keep her promise
he went to sleep in Christ, or as some
say, he died.

Then his mama, weeping that her
child was gone, yet glad that he was free
from pain and tears, remembered her
promise. So she went to Angel's own

little purse, and took out the money and bought a wax doll, and sent it to Cherub, saying, that an angel had given it to her.

Cherub took the doll in her arms, and sang sweet songs to it, and talked about Angel, and began to think of heaven.

Soon after Cherub became ill of the same disease that took away Angel. She often asked for her doll, and while she had breath, sang, with her clear, rich voice, until our hearts knew not which most to feel, delight or dread.

When she was dying, she said, to one who loved her,—

"Will you give me a beautiful blue dress?

And he said.—

"God is making a beautiful dress for you, my child."

So the lovely creature's spirit went to meet Angel's, and she was laid, meek and peaceful, in her coffin, and knew tears no more.

Then those who loved her, thought, "What shall we do with Angel's doll? no one should have it but Cherub."

So they took the doll, and laid it softly in Cherub's arms, in the coffin, and its red cheeks and bright eyes were pillowed near the pale, calm face of the child.

They rest together in a tranquil grave-yard, and evergreens grow around them.

THE FALCON.

THE FALCON FAMILY.

THOSE diurnal birds of prey which can be trained for hunting are termed Nobiles, or Noble; and among them are almost all those which form the falcon or hawk tribe. They equal eagles in courage; and although they are inferior in size and strength, they are superior in docility, gentleness, and entire obedience to the commands of those who train them for use or amusement.

The beak of falcons is very strong, and much more curved than that of any other bird of prey; it is also shorter, and has a projection from each edge of the upper part, like a sharply pointed tooth. The wings are long, and end in a point on one side; which shape obliges these birds to fly in a slanting direction when the weather is calm, and if they wish to rise in a straight line, they are forced to fly against the wind. They do not seek dead prey, and pursue their game at full speed, falling down upon it perpendicularly with great swiftness. Old birds differ much from the young in plumage, and the colors are brown, white, black, and gray, and occasionally a reddish tint; the female is generally one-third larger than the male; the eye-brows of both project very much, which gives them a very peculiar appearance, and their eyes are remarkably brilliant. The size varies from that of a large cock to a pigeon; the legs are blue or yellow, and there is a great variety of shape in the spots and bands formed by the feathers.

In consequence of falconry, or hawking, having been in former times a sport among all classes in northern nations, many curious laws were made about the practice of it, as at this day we find for shooting, fishing, or hunting with dogs; and a great deal of money was spent in keeping and training these birds. In those days it was only thought necessary for a nobleman to understand hawking, hunting, and exercise of arms; and he might, if he pleased, leave study and

3

learning to those who were of a rank beneath his own, without being remarkable
for his ignorance. There are many old
portraits of noblemen and gentlemen,
and even ladies, (for they used to join in
the sport on horseback,) with falcons on
their wrists; and King Harold was re-
presented with a bird on his hand and a
dog under his arm. The chief falconer
was the fourth officer in rank at court,
at the time when Wales had its own
kings; but he was only allowed to take
three draughts a day out of his drinking
horn, for fear he should get tipsy and
neglect his birds.

The expenses of falconry being so enor-
mous, those who infringed the laws re-
specting it were often severely punished.

A.BOWEN.

THE COMMON FALCON,

From a very old book we learn, that to steal a hawk, or even its eggs when found by chance, in the time of Edward II., subjected a person to imprisonment, and to pay a sum of money. It was the same in the time of Queen Elizabeth, with the additions that the offender was obliged to find some one who would answer for his good behaviour for seven years; and if he could not procure any one to do so, he was forced to remain in prison for that period.

A thousand pounds are said to have been given for a set of hawks, although the birds were procured in England, Wales, Scotland, and Ireland; these large sums, therefore, must have been paid for the trouble of training them.

Occasionally they were brought from Norway, and were then so much thought of, that they were esteemed fit for a sovereign. King John had two given to him as a bribe for allowing a man to trade in cheese.

Among the different kinds used in sport, the Perigrine falcon was reckoned the best, and is now the only one kept for the purpose in England, and that very rarely. Henry II. is said to have sent for some of them every year into Pembrokeshire. It however lives in most of the northern parts of the earth, and its flight is so rapid, that there are few countries which it does not visit.

The Gyr falcon is one of the largest of the tribe; its legs and beak are yellow,

and it was formerly trained to catch
cranes, herons, and wild geese. The
Goshawk was also flown at the same
prey, but more especially at pheasants
and partridges. Among the smaller
trained species was the Kestril, which
nests in the holes of ruins, high towers,
or clefts of rocks; its chief food is field-
mice, and it is that hawk which we see
remaining a long time in the air in one
spot, fanning its wings and watching for
its prey. The Hobby, also a small species,
was taught to catch larks, and was thrown
from the hand near their haunts, when
the poor little creatures would crowd together and remain motionless from fear;
a net was then thrown over them, and
all were secured.

The Kite, the Sparrowhawk, the Hen-harrier, the Merlin, and the Buzzard, do not appear to have been used for sporting. The first builds its nests in large forests, and has a forked tail. It may be known in the air from all other birds by its smooth flight, for its wings scarcely seem to move, and it appears frequently to remain motionless for a time. There is an old saying, that when kites fly high it will be fair weather; and the famous Pliny, who lived in the last times of the ancient Romans, and wrote a great deal about birds, says that the invention of the rudder for steering boats and ships was taken from the motion of a kite's tail.

The Sparrowhawk is a great enemy to

THE KITE.

pigeons and partridges; and it and the
Hen-harrier are very destructive to poul-
try. When we hear a hen cackle, and
see her cower down upon the ground,
and anxiously cover all her chickens
with her wings, we may be sure that
one of these destroyers is in the neigh-
borhood. The Merlin, although small,
is a very courageous bird, flies low, and
skims along the tops of the hedges in
search of its prey; it kills partridges by
one stroke upon the neck.

The Buzzards are much less active
than other hawks, they eat frogs, lizards,
mice, rabbits, birds, worms, and insects;
and one of them, which frequents moors
and marshy places, never soars into the
air. It is a very voracious bird, and

kills many young ducks; its legs are
longer and more slender than those of
hawks in general, by which it is better
enabled to find its way through wet
places.

THE WINDOW PANE AT NIGHT.

" Oh, what is the matter, my child!
Your looks are most awfully wild,—
   Why leave off your usual play?
Not noisy, for I heard not a sound,—
Now you throw down your doll on the
      ground,—
   Do listen, my Maud, and obey.

" Here's plenty of light—as you see,
Though you'd play in the dark far from
      me,
   Behind the red curtain you ran,

But now you run frightened about,
Of the reason you leave me in doubt;
    Pray tell me the cause—if you can?"

"Papa, at the window I saw!—"
"An owl, I suppose, or jackdaw."
    "Oh, no, but a robber, I'm sure!
She stared at me full in the face!"
"What, one of the poor gipsy race?"—
    "Why, no, I can't say she look'd
        poor.

"Her face is as rosy as mine;
Her eyes are bright blue—and they
        shine,
    But yet she began to look pale,
And opening her mouth as if crying,
I felt as if *I*, too, was dying!"
    "Well, this is a wondrous tale!"

"O cruel papa, how you laugh!
As if 'twere a cow or a calf,
   That really *is* your belief.
Papa might, I think, believe *me*—
Do go to the window and see,
   Then send out and catch the young
     thief!"

He took little Maud in his arms,
And said "These are foolish alarms,
   The pretty '*young thief*' I have caught!
Come now to the window with me,
And then you will speedily see
   The wonder the window-glass wrought."

Quickly holding her up to the pane,
She saw the same face come again!
   And there was papa's face also!

Convinced now, she bashfully smiled,
The glass showed a sweet smiling child!
  "Then this is the case,
  I saw my own face!"
Which truth little Maud was most
  happy to know.